T0081630

Arranged and Recorded by Mike Schmidt

Recording credits:
Mike Schmidt – Banjo, Guitar, Bass
Bruce King – Mandolin, Guitar

PLAYBACK+
Speed • Pitch • Balance • Loop

To access audio visit:
www.halleonard.com/mylibrary

Enter Code
5972-1108-4465-5722

ISBN 978-1-4950-2702-4

HAL•LEONARD®
CORPORATION
7777 W. BLUEMOUND RD. P.O. BOX 13819 MILWAUKEE, WI 53213

Visit Hal Leonard Online at
www.halleonard.com

Performance Notes
By Mike Schmidt

Thank you for purchasing *Bluegrass Gospel*. This is a collection of play-along tunes intended for the intermediate to advanced player of the 5-string Bluegrass banjo.

The tunes in this book are presented in several different keys. Because a capo is used, they're still written in a G form. So, songs in the key of A are capoed at the second fret and still thought of and played in terms of G. Because of the style, there are lots of open strings required, so with a capo, the banjo player can pretty much think in terms of the keys of G and C. Of course there are exceptions, but this covers a lot of the music we play, and all of the tunes in this book. That said, remember that the performance notes make references to G and C position, even though we might be in another key. Knowing the chord numbers is good, too. You know, the I, IV, and V symbols.

I believe that an important part of learning any instrument is playing with others. This is important on any level. This book and accompanying audio are the answer. Each tune has two corresponding audio tracks; one with the full band so you can hear the banjo parts, and one without the banjo, so you can play along with the rest of the band. Because it's recorded, the band won't stop if you make a mistake. This trains you to keep going no matter what happens, just like you'd do in a performance. The band isn't going to stop, so you need to pretend it never happened and just keep going. This is a valuable ability.

Another thing to consider here is the rhythm and speed at which the banjo is being played. This is an intermediate to advanced-level book, but the recorded tunes are still a bit slower than you might ultimately play them. With that, comes an occasional, involuntary change to the rhythm of the notes. As written you are looking at mostly eighth notes; and as played, these all have equal value. This is true for medium and fast tempo tunes, but if you listen to a slower tune, you might notice that the player will tend to "swing" the note values slightly. By "swing," we mean that each pair of notes is played with a bit of a stagger. The first of the two is of slightly longer duration while the second is slightly shorter. If you read music, you might think of it as if each pair of notes is a dotted-eighth and a 16th note. It's easier to listen to the recording and feel it than to explain it in writing. Someone once said, "Talking about music is like dancing about architecture." I think that applies here. Listen to the recording for "How Great Thou Art." That should explain it much better than I can here.

Something to notice here, and in any written music, are the chords written above the staff. These are for the accompanists – guitar, mandolin, bass, whatever. Just because you see a given chord does not mean you, the lead player, should automatically put that chord position down on the neck. You're playing the melody and often play single notes through those chords. There are times when you will hold chord shapes (particularly when you're playing backup chops), but it's not a given in lead parts. Please keep this in mind.

Every tune in this book consists of two banjo parts, or "breaks," with a mandolin break between. The first banjo break is a bit easier and the second is a bit more challenging. When playing along with the recording, remember that you can substitute the first break for the second. The chords are the same, so as soon as you know the first break, you can start practicing with the recording. The backup chords are provided for the mandolin breaks, too!

Backup
As mentioned earlier, we also address some basic backup techniques in these arrangements. While not intended as a lesson book, this still warrants some discussion. Since there are typically no percussion instruments in a Bluegrass band, other instruments can, and do, take these roles. It depends on the band, but very often, you'll find the banjo and mandolin taking on the role of the snare drum when they're not taking a break, as you will

hear in the play-along audio. During their lead breaks, both the banjo and mandolin are playing lots of rapid-fire notes, usually two notes to each beat. When one of these instruments is playing a solo, the other can play upbeats, not only to give that backbeat rhythm, but literally to get out of the soloist's way. Some banjo players choose to continue playing rolls behind a lead mandolin part, but in my opinion, that can get cluttered and can distract from the lead player. In the play-along audio, when one instrument is playing a lead break, the other is playing the backbeat accompaniment. Believe me, as a banjo player, the other players will appreciate it if you choose to do upbeats rather than continuing to do rolls. You will see that, while I do write the backup parts here as upbeat chops, I'll occasionally throw in a tag lick at the end of a phrase, but still it's minimal.

There are three positions for a major chord on the banjo: a barre chord, a D-position, and an F-position. This means that you'd use the shape of a D or F chord, but on different frets to make different chords. A barre is simply putting one finger across all the strings on the same fret.

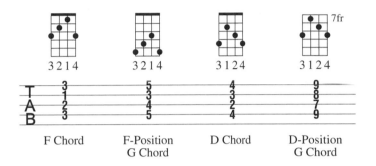

So, start by playing an F chord. If you move this up two frets, keeping the same finger position, it will become a G chord. A barre across the 5th fret is C, and on the 7th fret is D.

The backup parts written in this book are not etched in stone; they're suggestions. As long as you play the right chords, you're free to do anything you like. For example, if what's written alternates between two inversions (positions) of a given chord, feel free to just stay on one of those positions if it's more comfortable for you. If the book shows a bit of a tag lick at the end of a phrase and you'd rather play chops, go for it.

"Cryin' Holy unto the Lord"

Initially, there's nothing too unusual going on here. One thing I like to do a lot is to play a C chord, leaving the first string open; technically making it a Cadd9 chord. It's a good sound. In addition, that open D note on the first string is a common tone with G and D chords. I do this in measures 5 and 6, adding a 3rd fret to the 3rd string, making it a 7th chord. To my ear, it's a good sound.

As mentioned earlier in the Backup section, the banjo tab in this book is what was played on the recording, but that doesn't mean you need to play it exactly that way. In a tune that's capoed a bit higher, like this one, I might stay with the F-position G-type chords, because they're already getting kind of high up the neck, but you might consider starting the mandolin break by alternating between the F- and D-position chords, like what's happening in measure 28. This is purely up to you.

The second banjo break starts at measure 36, but not with the first note. Actually, this break starts with the 2-3 slide as a pickup to measure 37.

Probably the main thing to pay attention to throughout this song is the syncopated rhythms found in measures 9, 14, 41, 42, 45, 47, and 50. While they're written out correctly, sometimes it's best to just use the tab to get the correct notes, and use your ear to get the rhythm.

"How Great Thou Art"

This is a medium tempo tune without too many bumps, and the tempo makes any tricky spots a bit easier. Throughout, you'll find interesting things like hammer-ons that start by picking two strings together, and then hammering one on. A good example is the very beginning. That same move happens again in measures 8, 64 and 72.

Another interesting one is a triplet, which happens twice in the song; at measure 10, and with a slight variation in measure 67. In measure 10, notice that there are three notes on the "and" of beat 2 (in cut-time). This is a triplet, meaning three notes are played evenly on that upbeat. To make it a bit more challenging, you pick the first note (1st string open) with the middle finger, then hammer it on and immediately pull it back off. In measure 10, I suggest using your ring finger to fret the 2nd fret of the first string because in the next measure, you will be doing basically a C chord. This way, you're a step ahead.

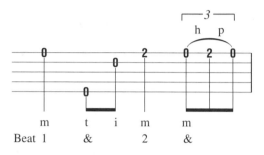

A similar move happens in the third measure of the second banjo break; measure 67 to be exact. You start that measure by picking the 2nd string with the index finger, then a pinch with a hammer-on to the 2nd fret of the 1st string, making it a C chord position. The second beat of this measure begins by picking the first string open, then hammering it onto the 2nd fret and pulling it back off – triplet sixteenth notes and one eighth note. This is possibly easier if you hear it and feel it than if you try to count it out. Also, if this doesn't work, you can hold the previous hammer-on and just play the 2nd fret and pull it off as two eighth notes.

Notice measure 21. It's labeled as a D chord, but you're playing a D7 along with the 4th fret of the first string. Either chord would work, they're both a form of D, and the melody note is covered on the third string. But I like the voicing of the D7 with that high F#. If, on the other hand, you played a straight D major here, it would work equally well.

In the backup, measure 42 is easier than it looks. The first chord is a D-position G chord. The next group of notes is simply an F-position on the same three frets; essentially trading the index and middle finger positions (making it a B). The remainder is simply right hand. Playing the B and sliding the whole chord up one fret for that final "10" of that measure, where it becomes the C chord for measure 43.

In the ending, you have a two-measure upward run. The 5th frets can be covered with a brief barre chord, as can the 7th frets. For the 9th and 10th frets of the first and second strings, fret those with the index and middle fingers respectively, and catch the fifth string, 10th fret with the thumb. Finish it with a pair of 12th fret harmonics on the first and second strings, and you're done.

"I Saw the Light"

Starting at Section B, measures 18 and 19 have an interesting rhythmic pattern going. In this two-measure pattern, there are four hammer-ons but they're not in the usual two-16ths-and-an-eighth pattern. They're straight eighth notes, and all are picked with the index finger. Then, when the pull-off comes in measure 19, it's back to the "normal" rhythm with the sixteenth notes.

Measure 86 consists of a pair of 2-3 slides. I play them this way because I'm used to it… muscle memory. I do, however, like the sound of a hammer-on here and when I'm thinking ahead enough, I try to use that move instead of the slide; it seems to emphasize the notes a bit more. Just something to think about.

"I'll Fly Away"
The first thing to point out happens early in the mandolin break. We start at measure 33 with backup chops, alternating between F- and D-position. In measure 36, notice the second chord. First of all, we're in the key of A, but because we have a capo, we're thinking in terms of G; so when I name a chord, I'm thinking that way. A IV chord here is referred to as a C because, for all practical purposes that's what the banjo is doing. The fact that it sounds like a different chord is not pertinent to what we're talking about.

Anyway, from the beginning of the mandolin break, we were alternating between inversions of the I (G) chord. The first chord of measure 36 is still a G, but the second chord is a D-position F. Why? Because the F note is the flat-7 note in a G7 chord, which is a leading tone to the C chord that's about to happen. Normally you might play a G7 chord to anticipate the C, but here, if everyone else is still playing their G or G7, and YOU play an F chord, it really sets it off. That's a lot of explanation for half of a beat, but it's a nice touch if you don't over-use it.

Measures 51 through 54 are a nice way to move from the I to the IV. Yes, it's rolling backup instead of chops, but it eventually gets back to the chops. At measure 51, begin with just the pinky fretting the first string, 3rd fret. Keeping that down, use the middle finger for the 2 on the third string. In measure 52, continue holding the pinky down while you use the index for the 1 and ring for the 3. In measure 53, you're now doing the IV (C) position without fretting the first string. Start with index fretting the second string, and go from there, as written.

The second banjo break is pretty heavily melodic, full of step-wise, up-the-neck material but it's fun. The challenging part is that, ultimately, you might want to play this half-again-as-fast as it is in the recording. Starting at measure 81, for the chorus of the banjo break, you go way up the neck. You're using the middle and index fingers of the left hand on the 10 and 9 in measure 81, and the 15 and 14 in measure 82. The notes on the fifth string are fretted with the thumb. Also, that 17th fret of the first string is done by extending the pinky while holding the other fingers in the position they were already in.

Later, in measure 89, there are a few fretted notes on the fifth string as well. Again, these are fretted with the thumb.

"I'll Have a New Life"
There's a little thing I like to do when moving from an A-position to a D-position (II to V). This happens in measures 6 and 7. For the A-position, do a normal barre chord across the 2nd fret with the index finger. But when you change to the D-position, don't lift the index. Instead, just add the middle and pinky to make it a D, keeping the index down as the barre. It's quicker than lifting the index and putting it right back down. The same chord change happens in the second banjo break, at measures 42 and 43. It's counted differently, so you can elect to do the same thing you did for measures 6 and 7 or, since you have more time, you can lift the A-position and do a regular D.

In measure 40, there's a 0-2 hammer-on played and counted as straight eighth notes, but watch the last note of 40. It's picked, but the first note of the next measure is hammered onto a quarter note. It's an interesting effect.

Finally in measure 47 (I mentioned this earlier in "I Saw the Light.") is the option of slides versus hammer-ons. In the recording for this tune, I played hammer-ons (however I'm more inclined to do slides in this situation). I think you can hear the difference. So again, it's written as hammer-ons, but slides work very well in this particular situation.

"Man in the Middle"

The verse and chorus to this tune are different, but the breaks throughout are verses only, so that's what we have here. We did not deal with the chorus in this arrangement.

This tune had an interesting little bump in it, causing us to write it a bit differently from the others. Notice that every song in this collection is written in cut time. If you're unfamiliar with cut time, it's notated exactly as it would be in 4/4, but you play it as though the note values were cut in half, giving the half note the beat rather than the quarter. This song is handled the same except for one thing: in each verse, there's a 1-beat measure –a half measure if you will. So, in counting, when you'd normally be counting 1 - 2, 1 - 2, here, you'll be doing a 1 - 2, 1, 1 - 2, 1 - 2, or if it's easier, 1 - 2 - 3, 1 - 2, 1 - 2. Once you hear the recording, it should make sense.

Other than that, there are several spots where you'll use the same picking finger multiple times in a row. This tune isn't that fast, so it's not really a problem.

"Turn Your Radio On"

This happens occasionally in the book: there will be a figure like the one found in measure 4, where there are three notes in a row on the fourth string. Notice we see a 2-0-2 figure picked with thumb, index, thumb. At first it seems a bit tricky, but I usually don't do something like this if it's a fast tune. This one is medium speed, so shouldn't be too bad. This happens again in measure 20.

There's a similar move in measure 16, but it's on the first string, and involves two consecutive picks of the first string with the middle finger. Again, the medium tempo of this tune makes it easier to do. This happens again in measures 22 and 80.

One possible tricky spot is in measure 87.

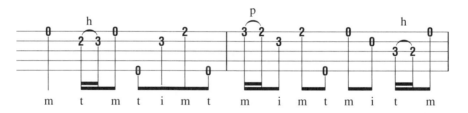

This is really a reworking of the pattern shown above; same left hand movement, but the timing is a bit different. If measures 87 and 88 prove difficult, you can use what's shown here in its place.

"Wicked Path of Sin"

The backup is pretty straightforward here. Because the recording is in the key of C (G-position, capoed on the 5th fret), I tend to start with the F-position I chord. Getting to the D-position when capoed up this high seems a bit high-pitched for my tastes. It's not wrong, and I do occasionally go between the two (measures 35 - 38) but I tend to avoid it in the higher keys. As always, you are free to do whatever you like in the backup, what's shown here is purely suggestion.

Toward the end of the mandolin break (measure 62), you'll see two chords on the downbeats. It's the suspended-V chord, resolving to a V. Straight V chord upbeats would be perfectly fine here.

The two eighth notes that start measure 64 are worth noting. The first note ends the mandolin break while the second begins the second banjo break. With that in mind, I'd accent that second eighth note (picked with the index finger) just a bit to set it off.

Cryin' Holy unto the Lord

Words and Music by Irene Amburgey Roberts

G tuning:
(5th-1st) G-D-G-B-D

Key of B
Capo IV

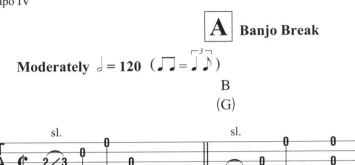

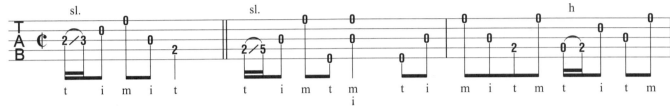

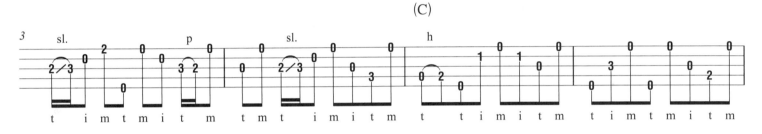

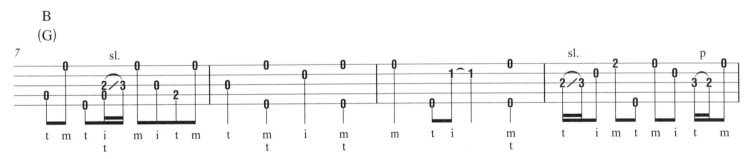

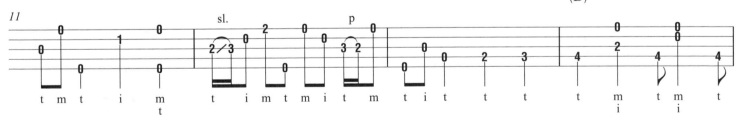

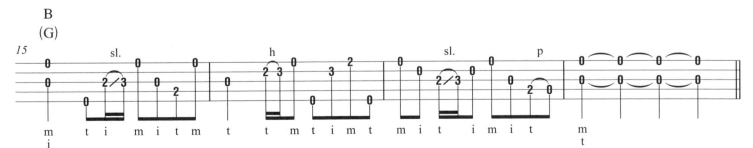

Mandolin Break

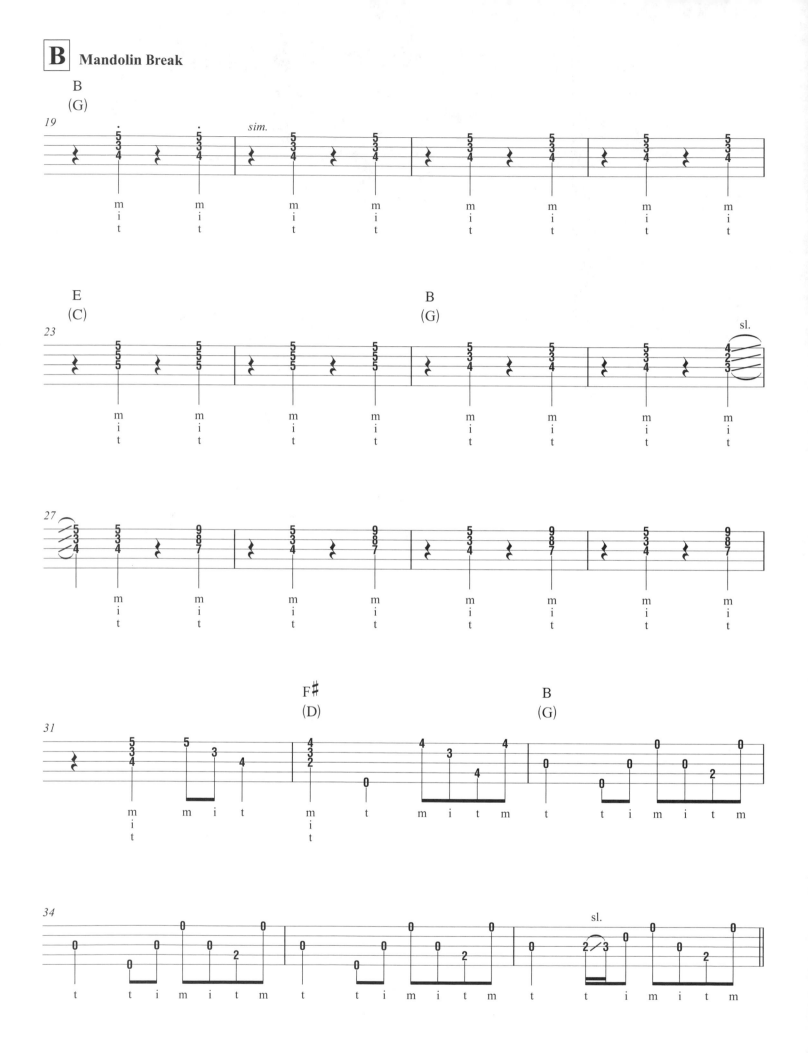

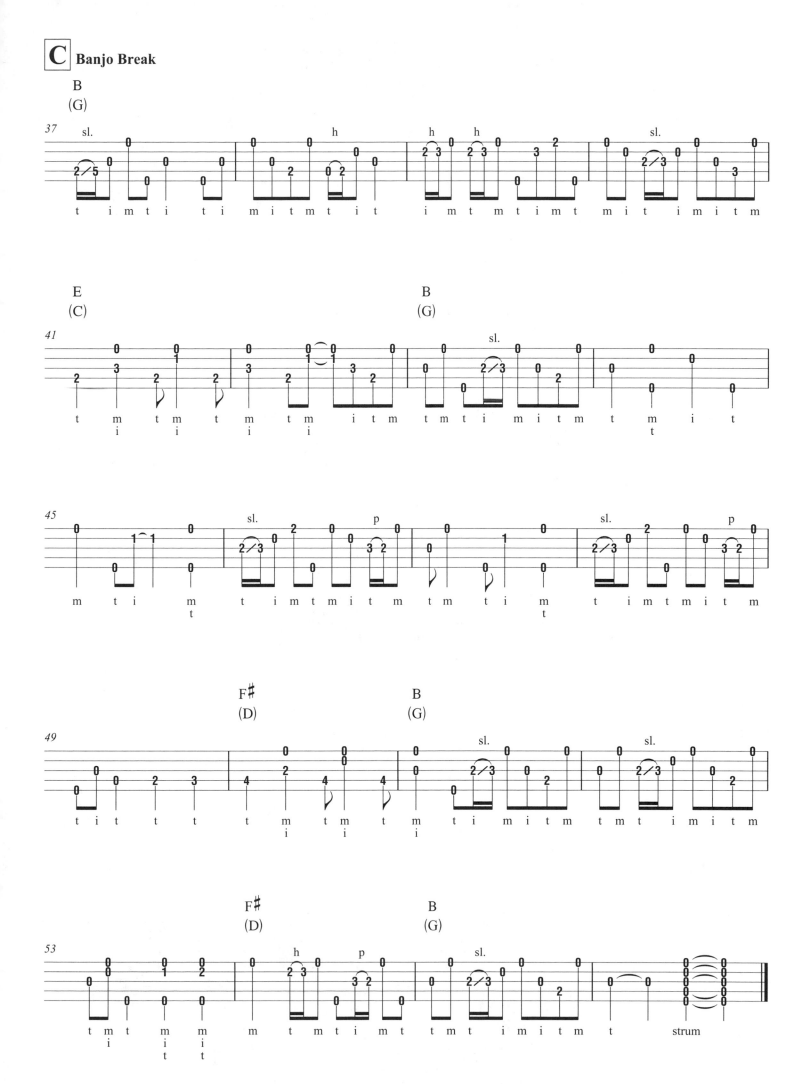

How Great Thou Art

Words by Stuart K. Hine
Swedish Folk Melody Adapted and Arranged by Stuart K. Hine

G tuning:
(5th-1st) G-D-G-B-D

Key of G

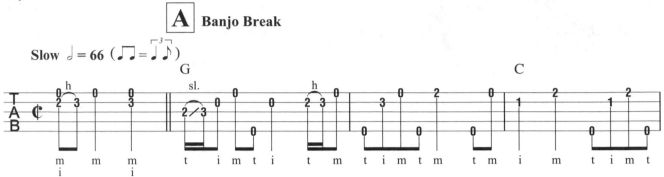

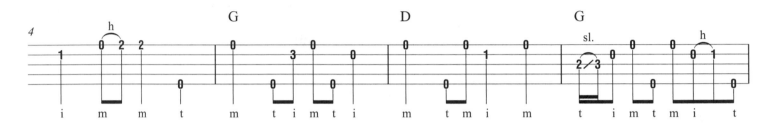

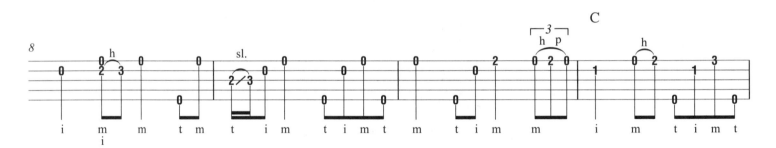

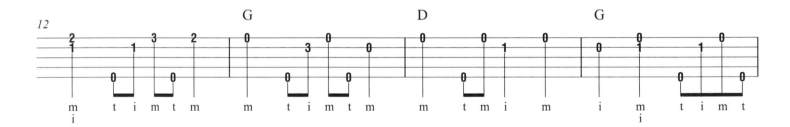

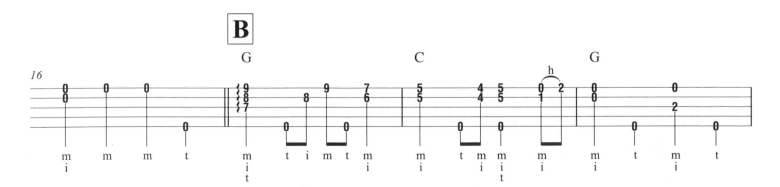

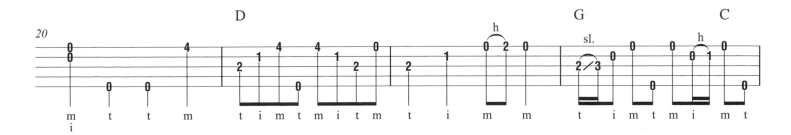

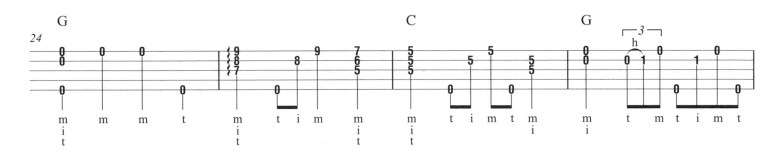

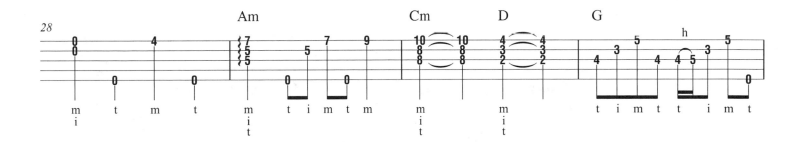

C Mandolin Break

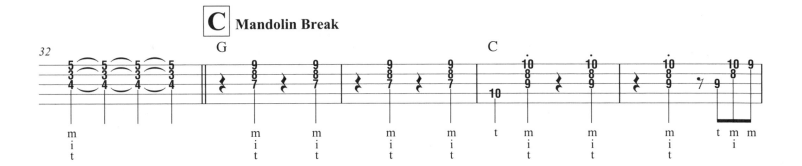

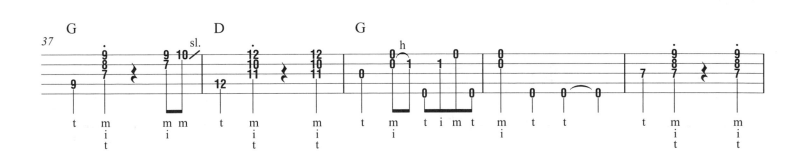

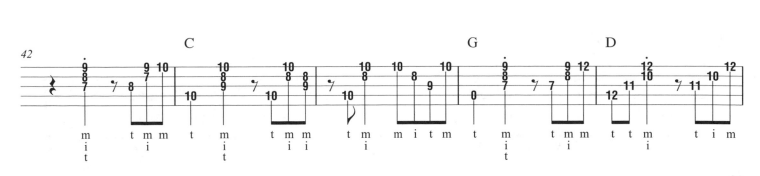

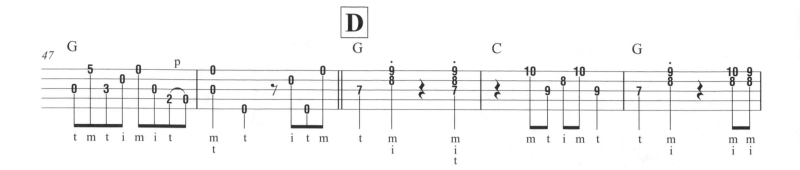

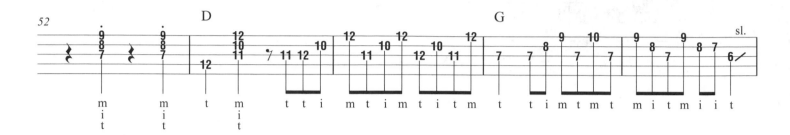

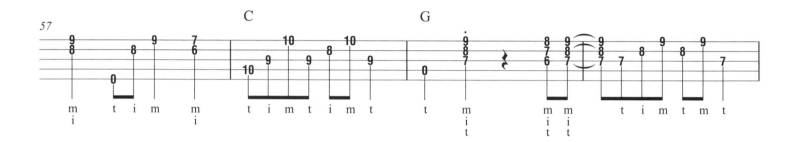

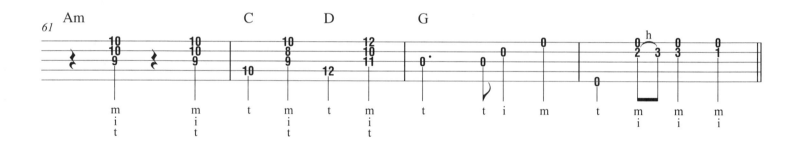

E **Banjo Break**

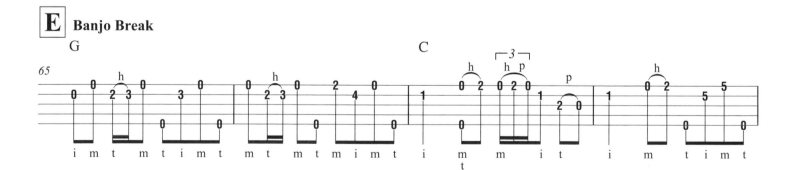

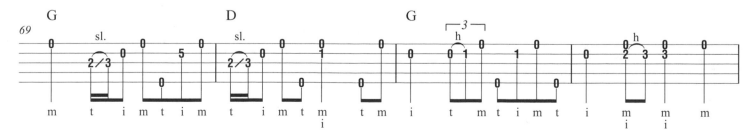

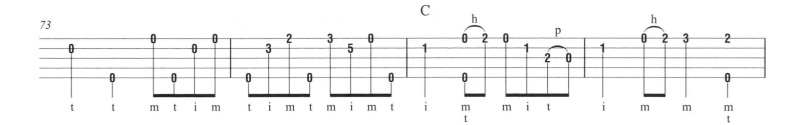

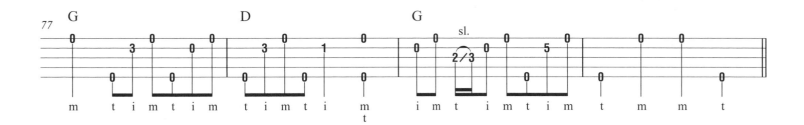

F

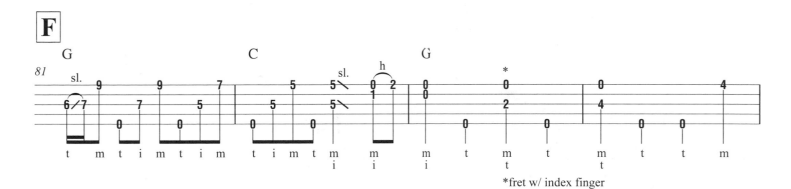

*fret w/ index finger

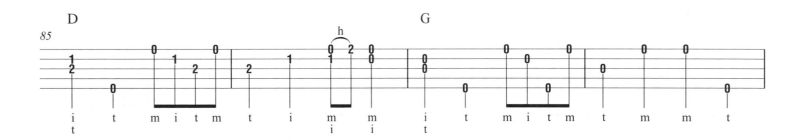

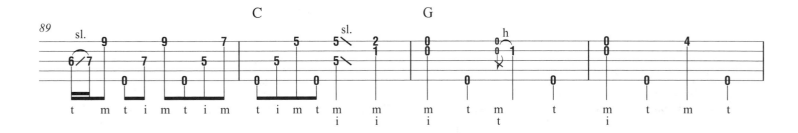

Slower

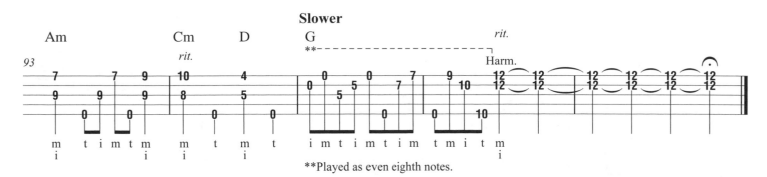

**Played as even eighth notes.

I'll Have a New Life

Words and Music by Luther Green Presley

G tuning:
(5th-1st) G-D-G-B-D

Key of A
Capo II

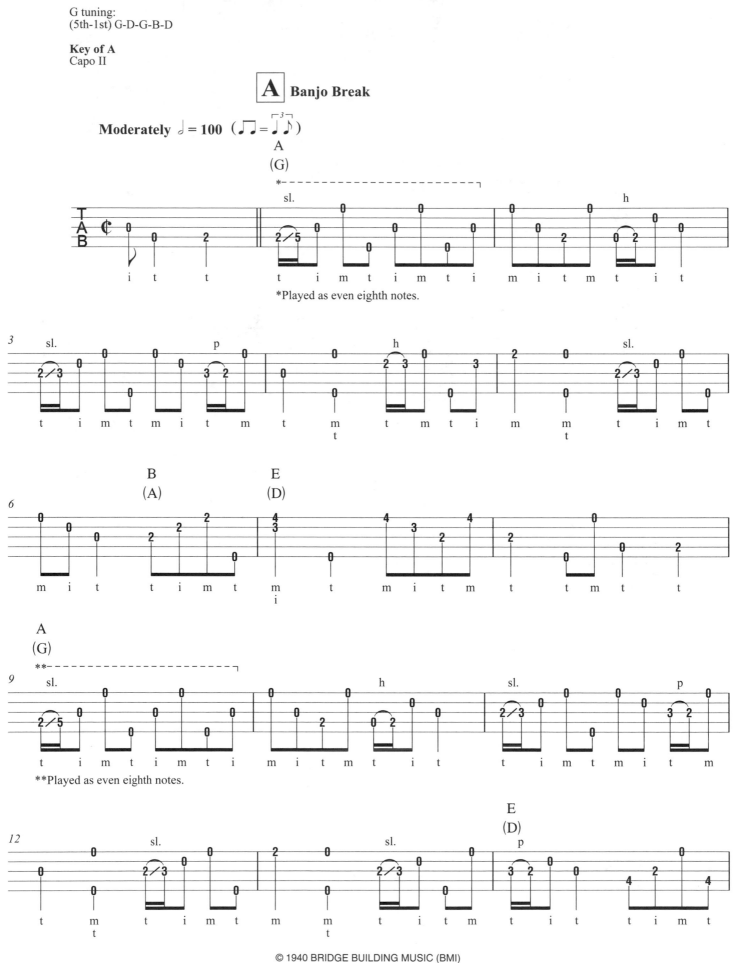

*Played as even eighth notes.

**Played as even eighth notes.

B Mandolin Break

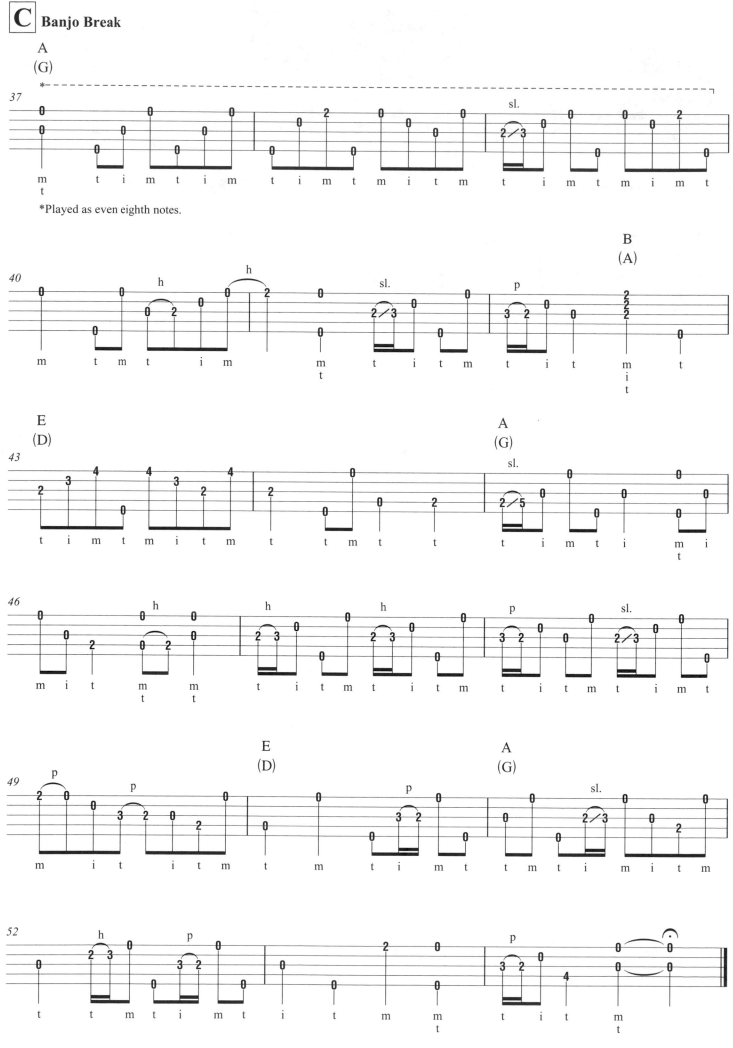

*Played as even eighth notes.

I Saw the Light

Words and Music by Hank Williams

G tuning:
(5th-1st) G-D-G-B-D

Key of A
Capo II

 **Banjo Break**

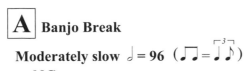

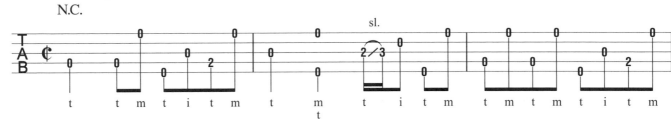

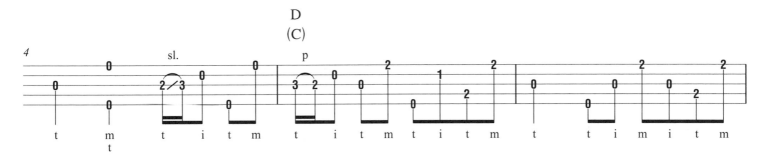

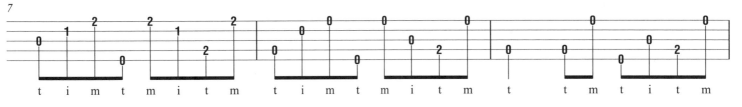

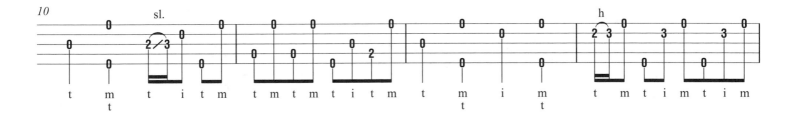

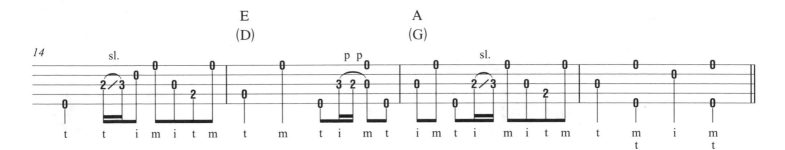

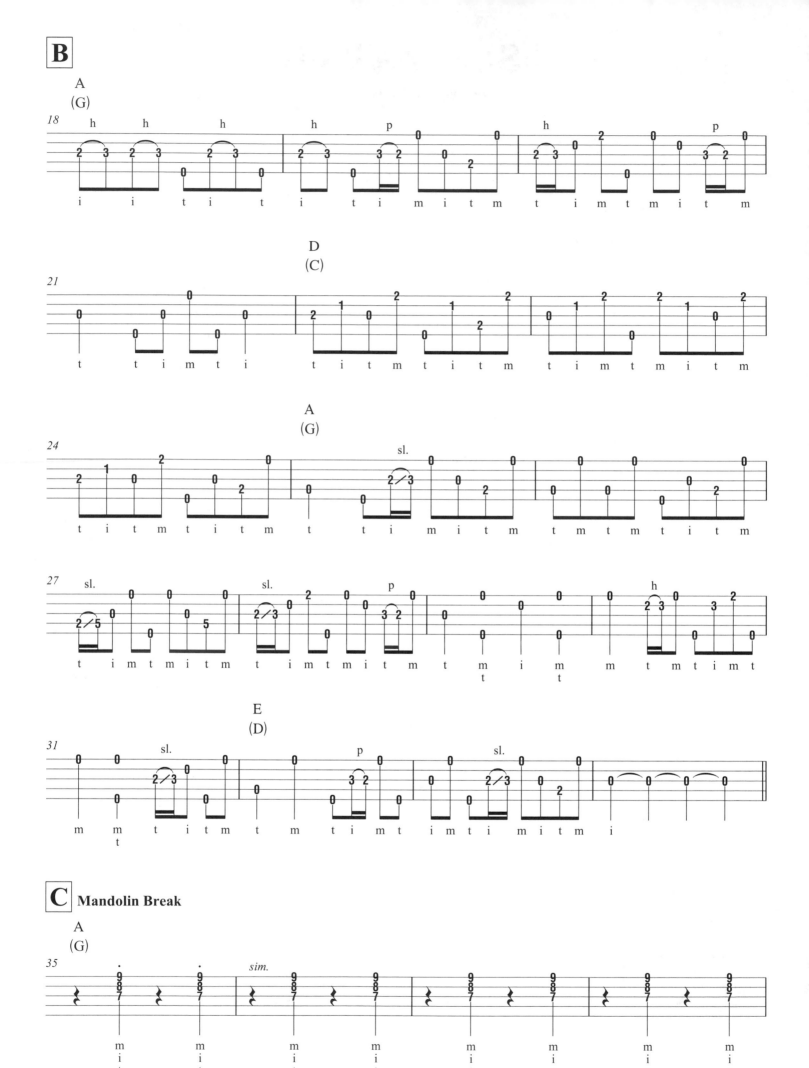

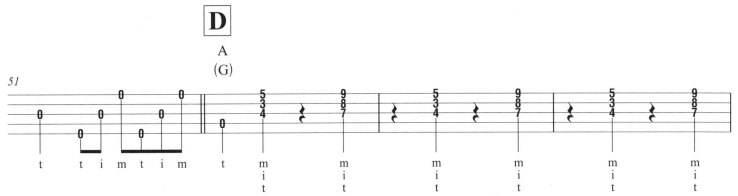

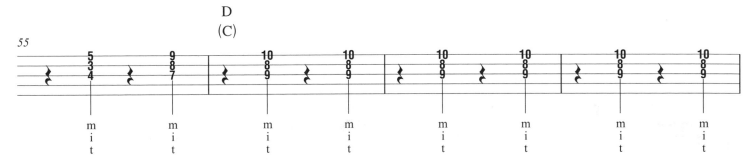

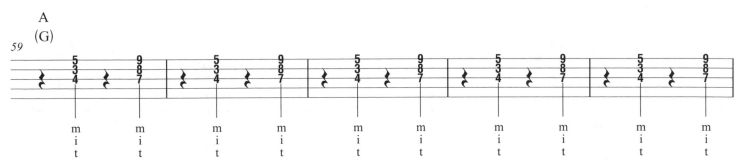

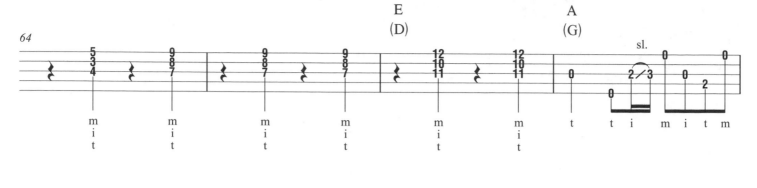

E Banjo Break

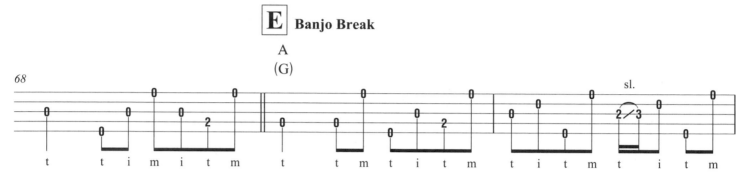

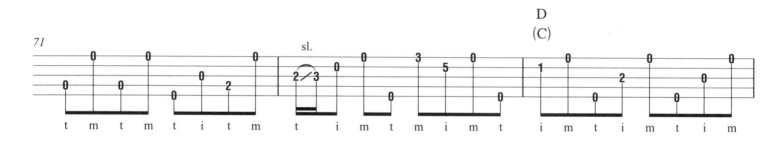

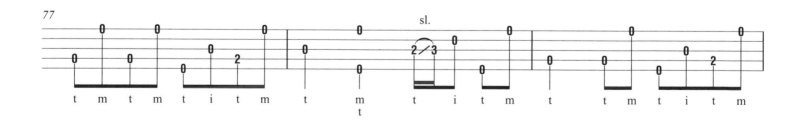

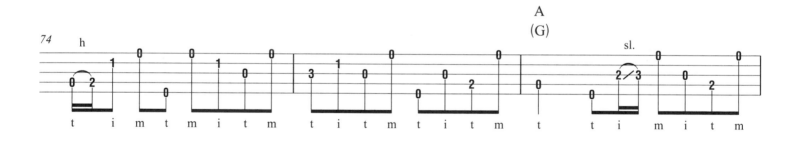

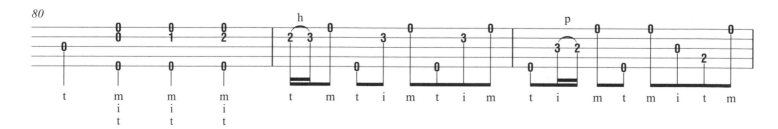

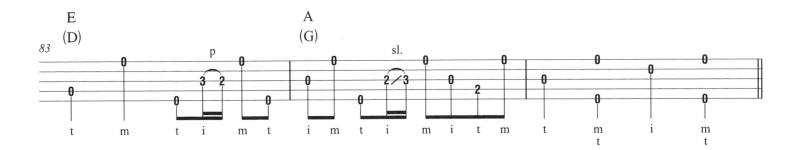

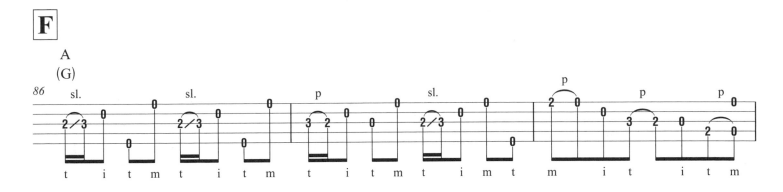

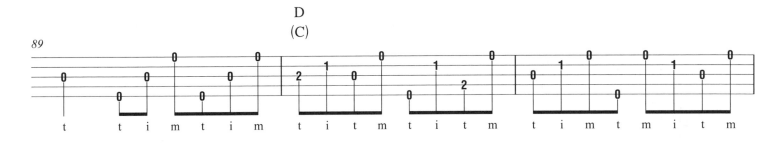

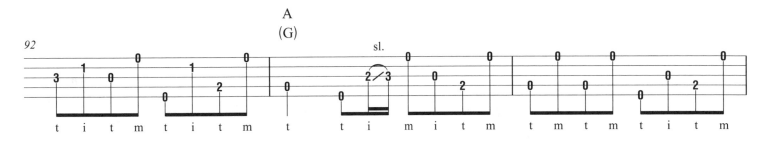

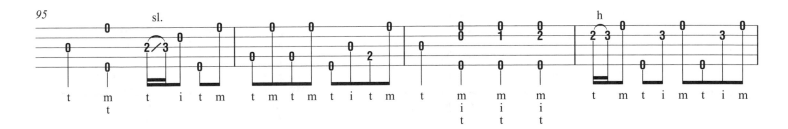

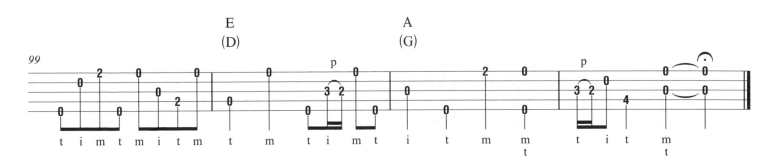

I'll Fly Away

Words and Music by Albert E. Brumley

G tuning:
(5th-1st) G-D-G-B-D

Key of A
Capo II

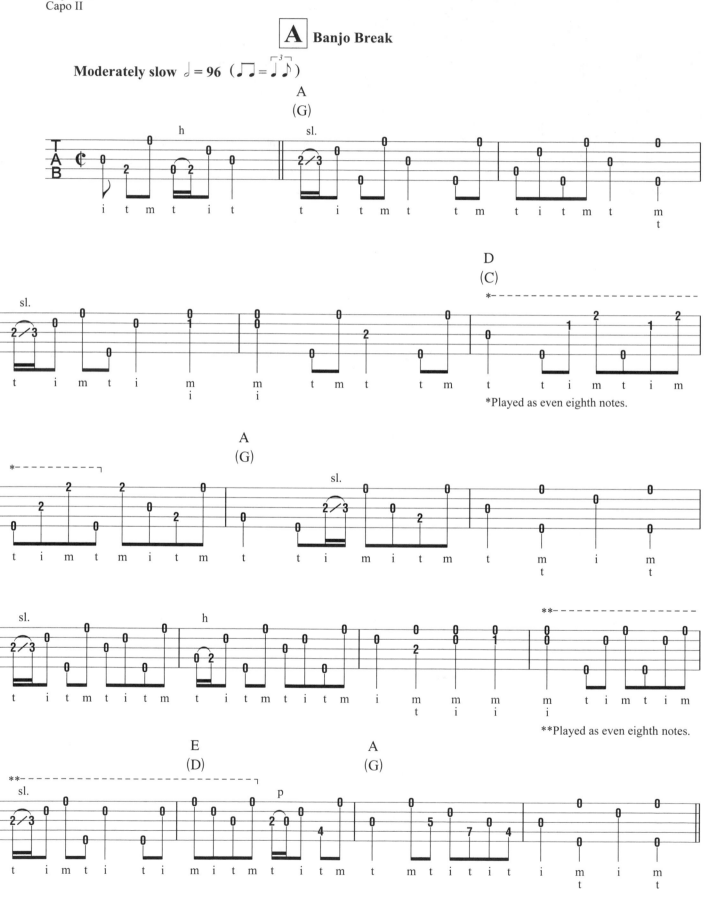

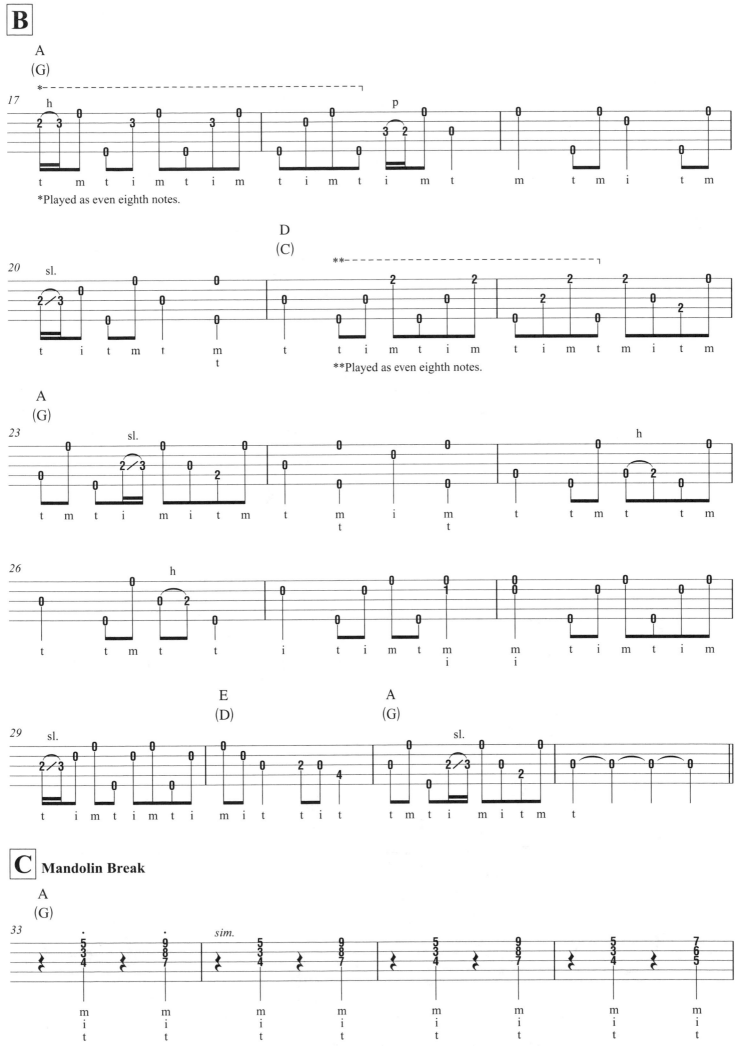

*Played as even eighth notes.

**Played as even eighth notes.

C Mandolin Break

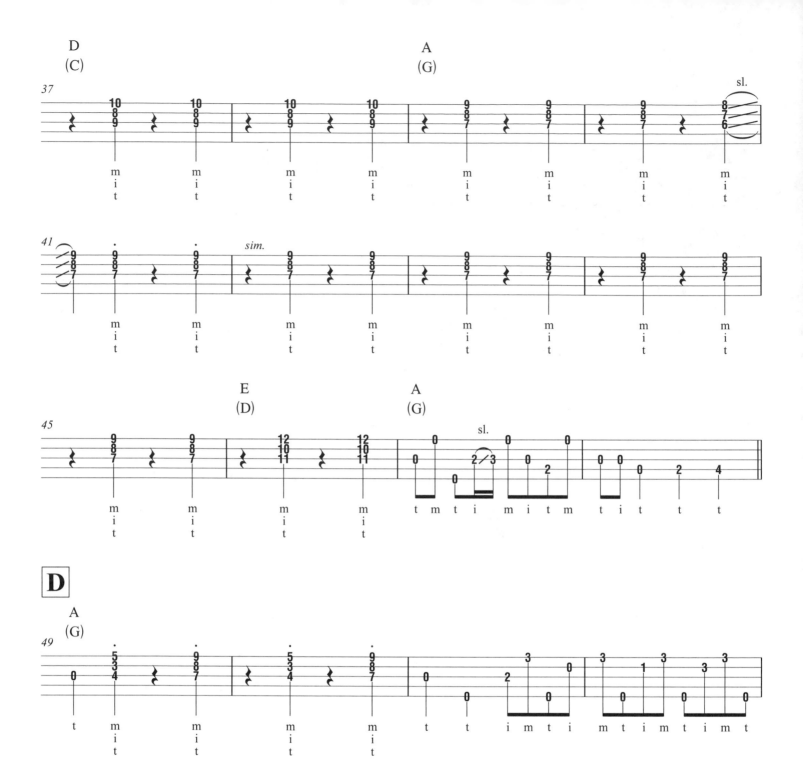

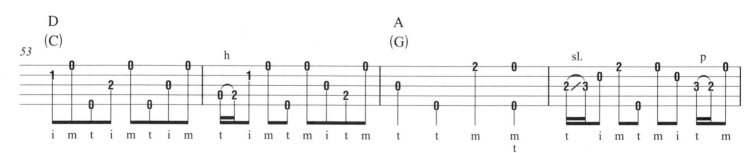

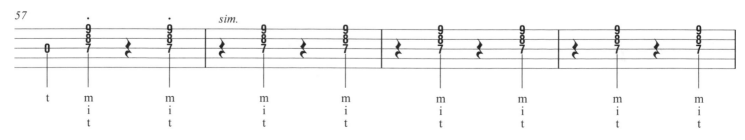

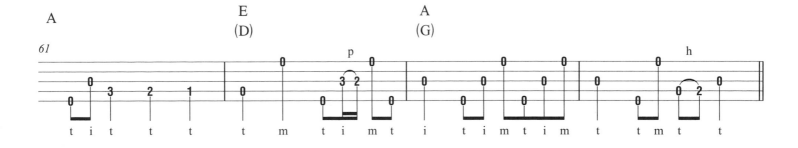

E Banjo Break

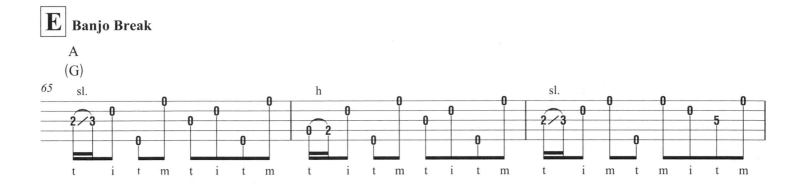

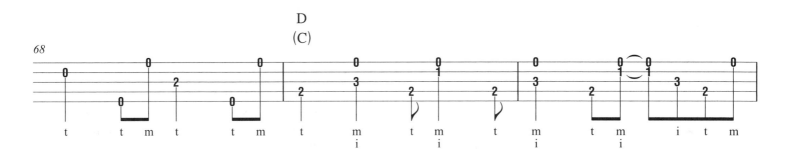

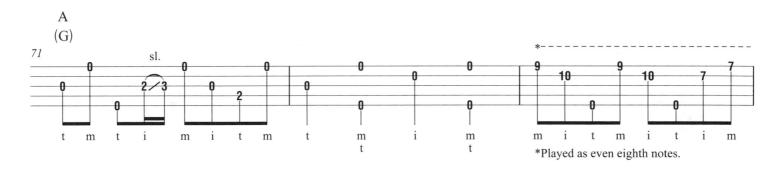

*Played as even eighth notes.

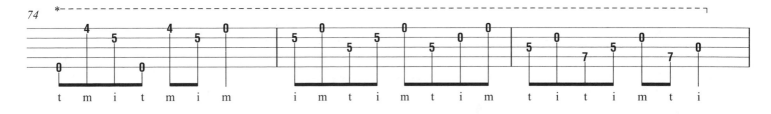

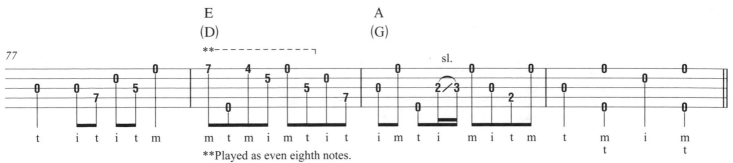

**Played as even eighth notes.

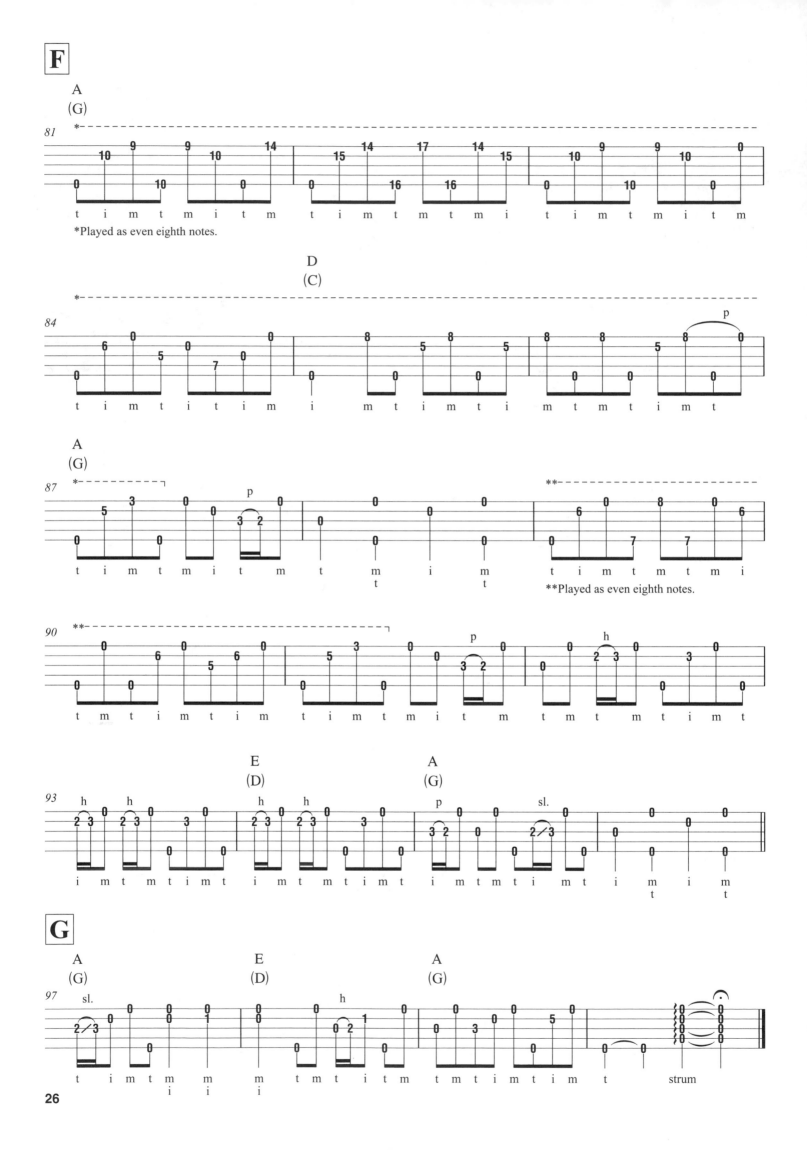

*Played as even eighth notes.

**Played as even eighth notes.

Man in the Middle

Words and Music by Thomas E. Campbell

G tuning:
(5th-1st) G-D-G-B-D

Key of G

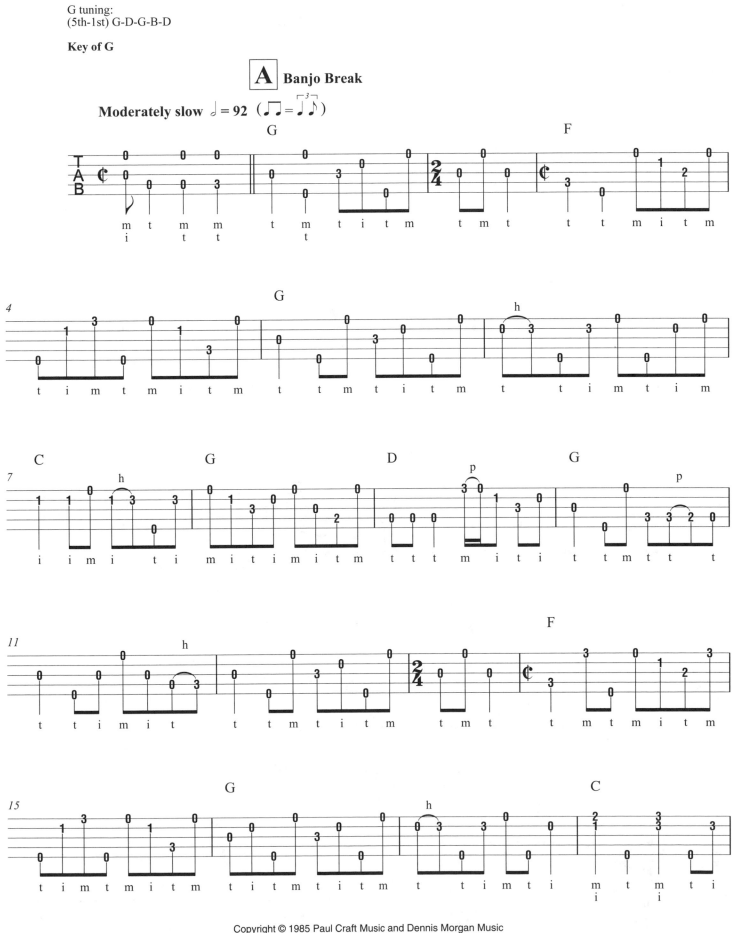

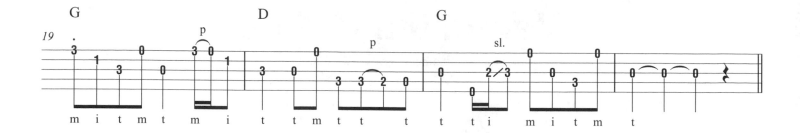

B Mandolin Break

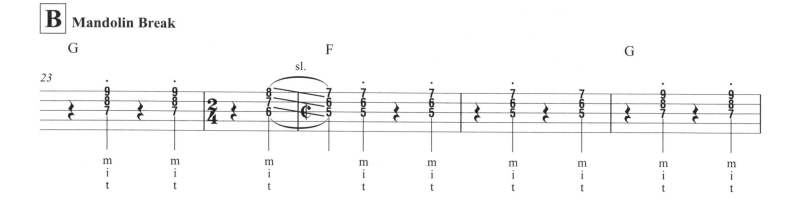

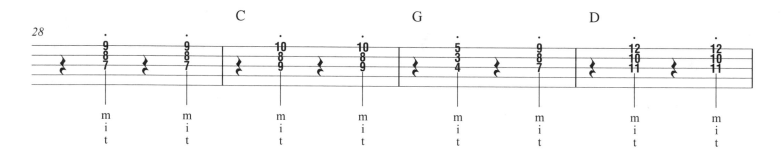

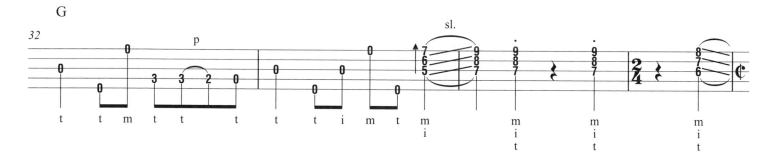

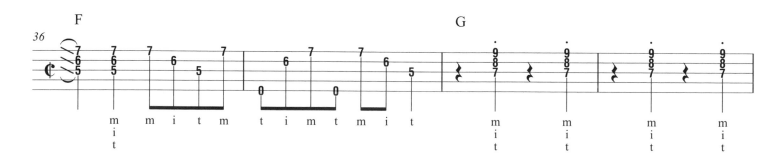

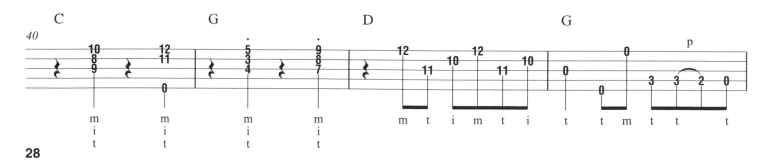

28

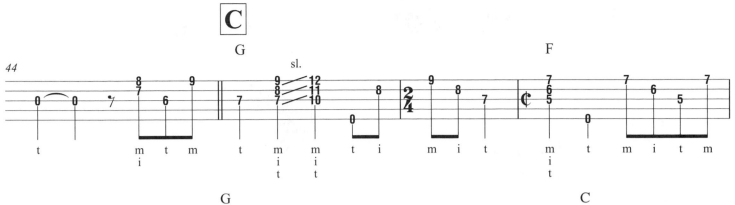

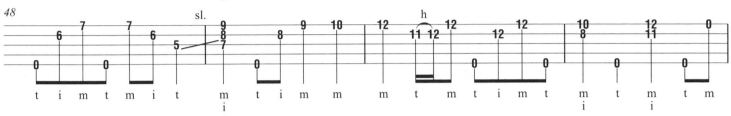

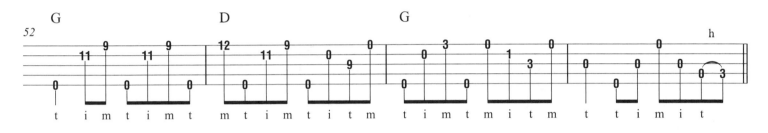

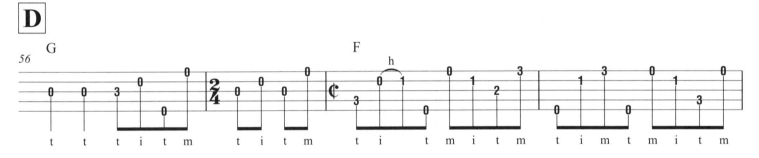

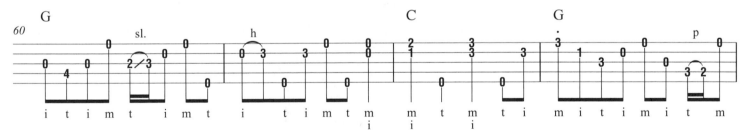

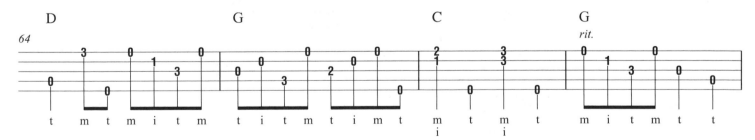

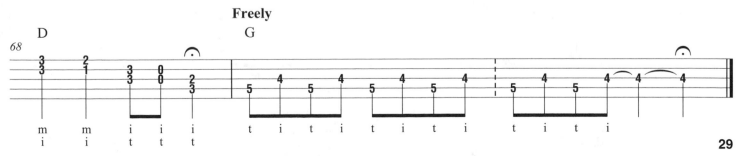

Turn Your Radio On

Words and Music by Albert E. Brumley

G tuning:
(5th-1st) G-D-G-B-D

Key of G

A **Banjo Break**

Moderately ♩ = 100

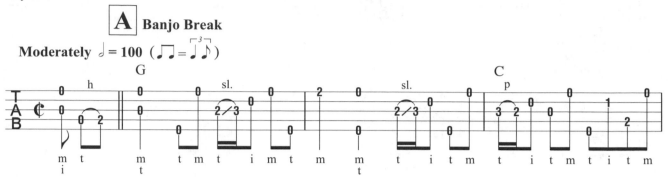

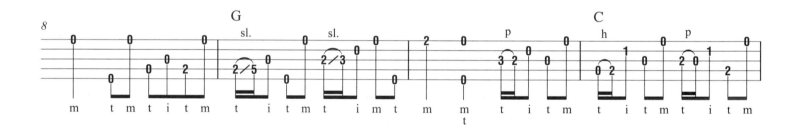

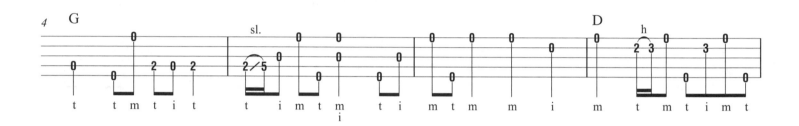

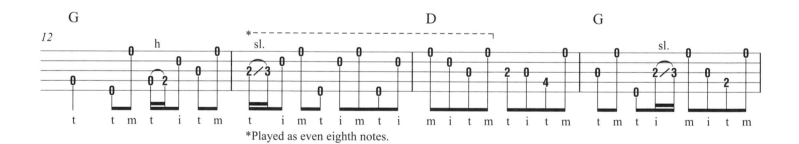

*Played as even eighth notes.

B

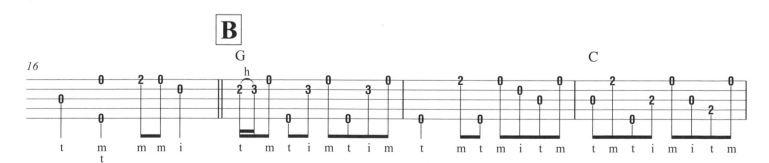

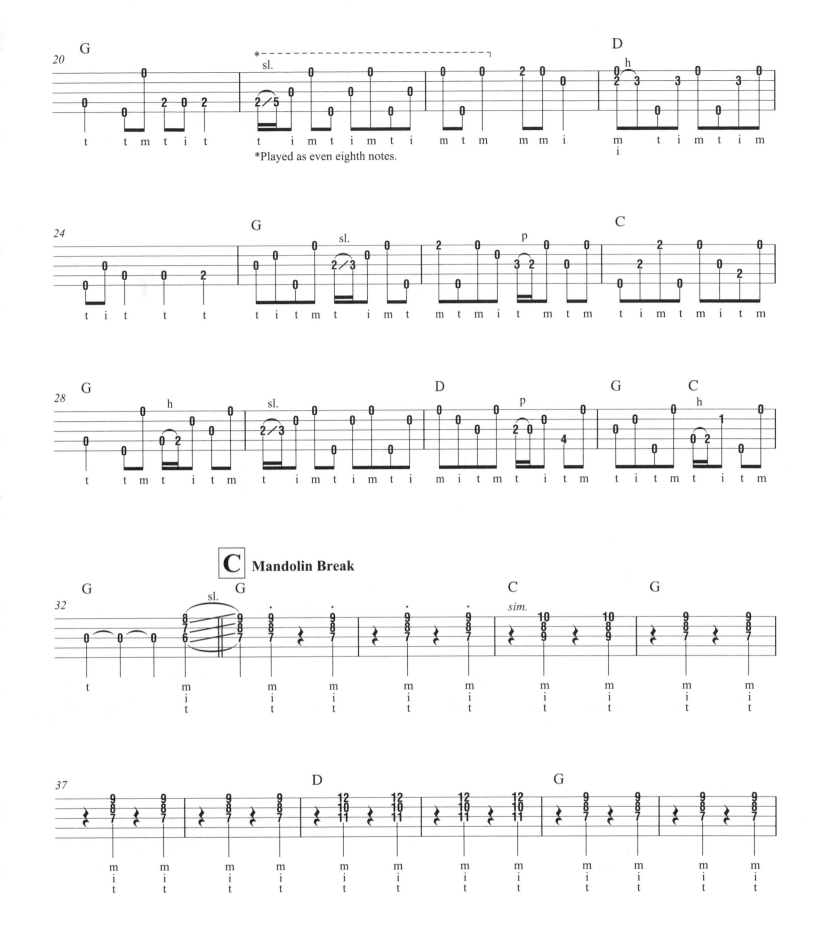

*Played as even eighth notes.

C Mandolin Break

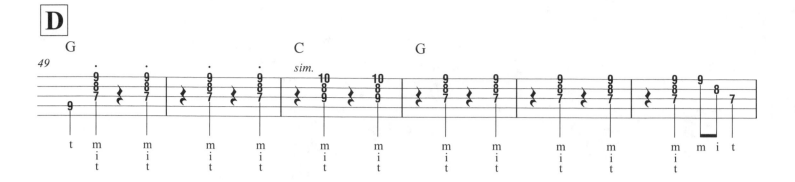

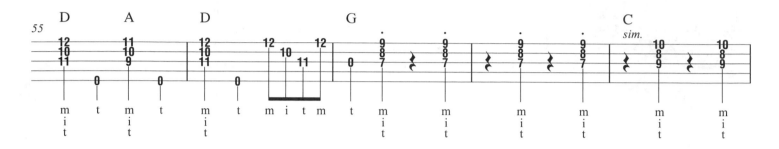

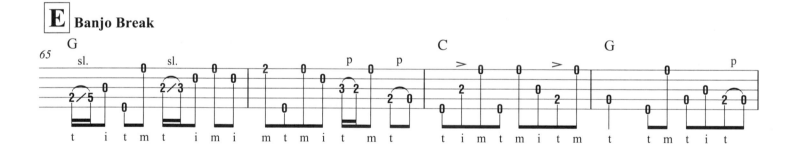

E Banjo Break

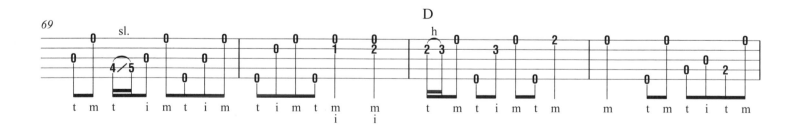

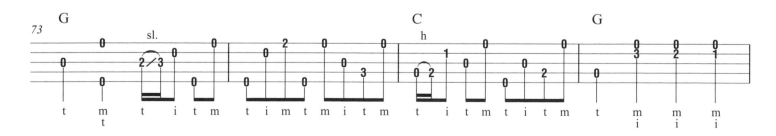

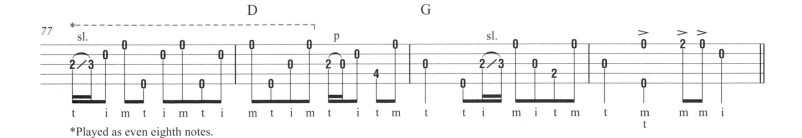

*Played as even eighth notes.

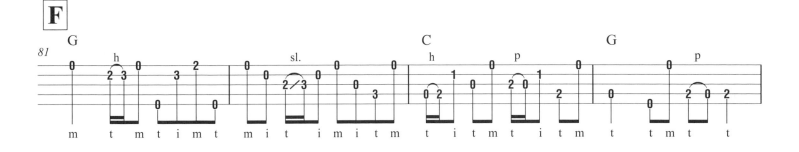

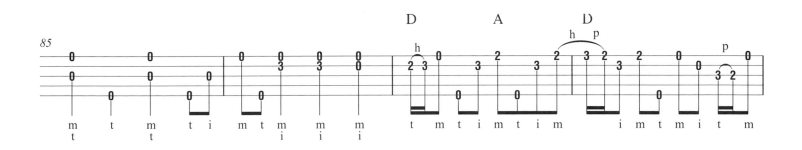

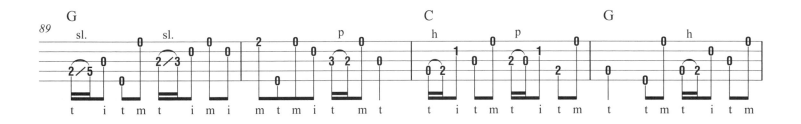

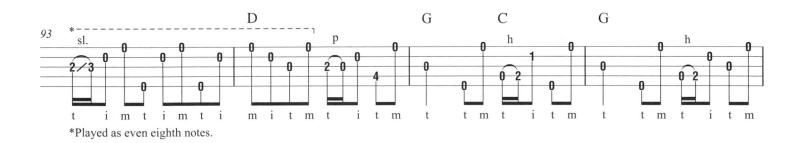

*Played as even eighth notes.

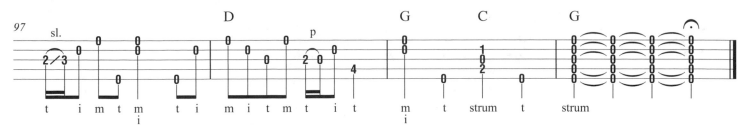

Wicked Path of Sin

Words and Music by Bill Monroe

G tuning:
(5th-1st) G-D-G-B-D

Key of C
Capo V

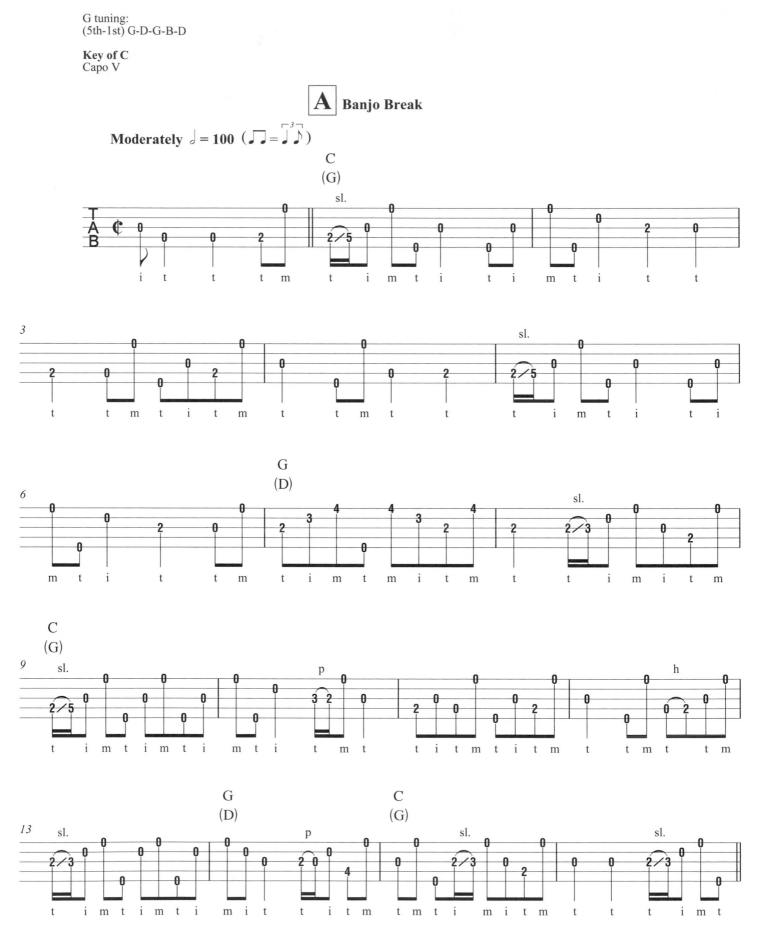

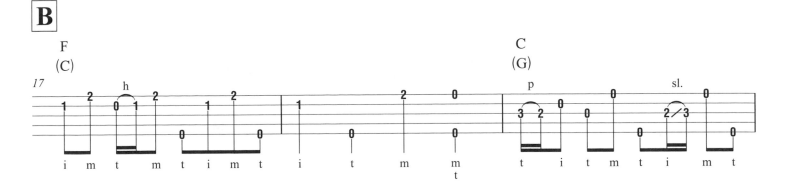

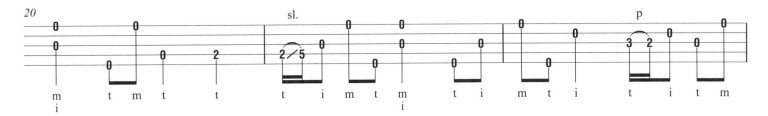

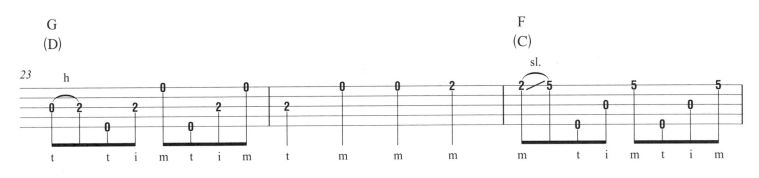

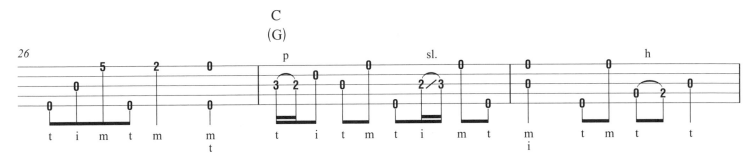

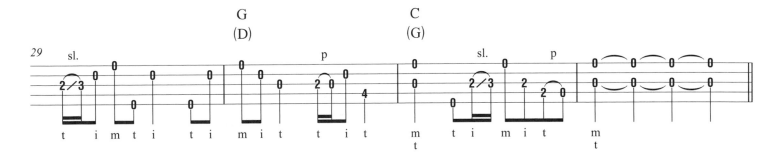

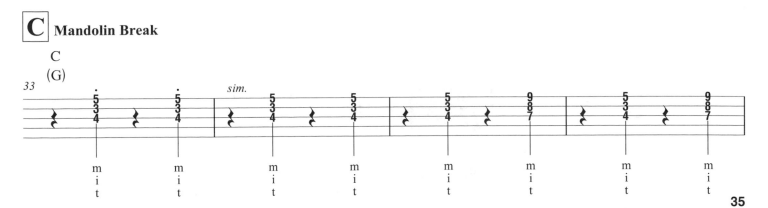

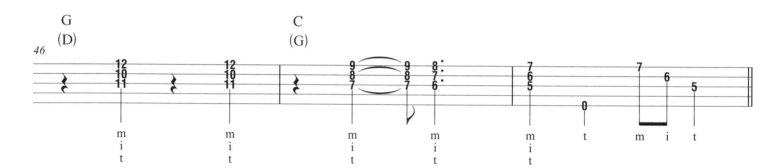

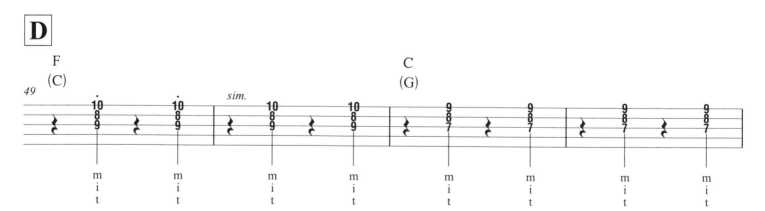

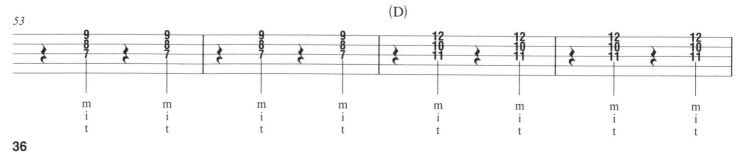

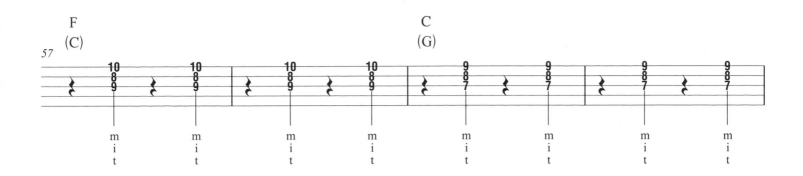

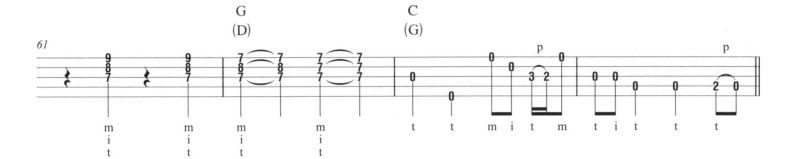

E Banjo Break

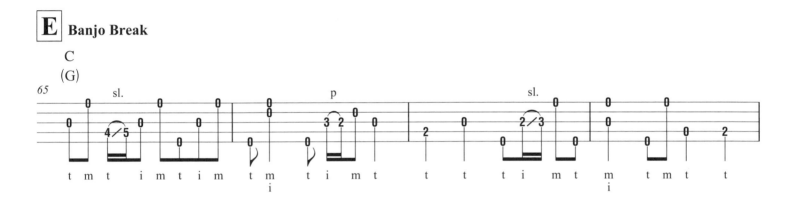

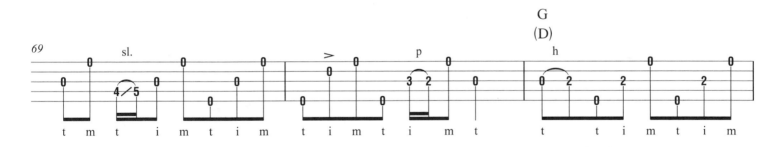

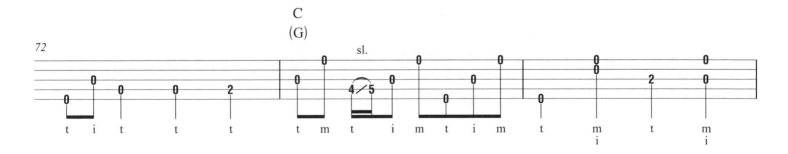

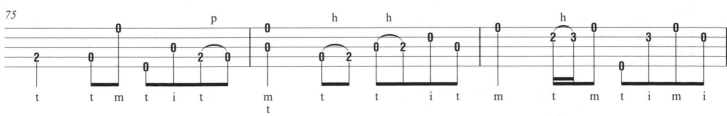

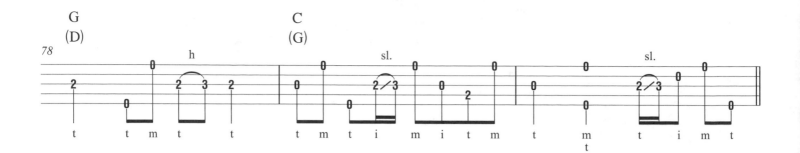

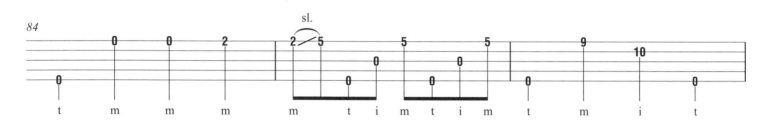

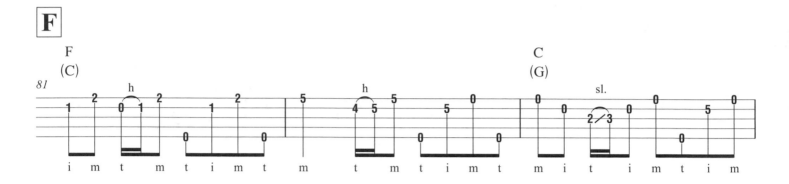

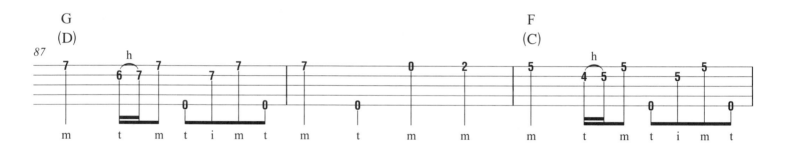

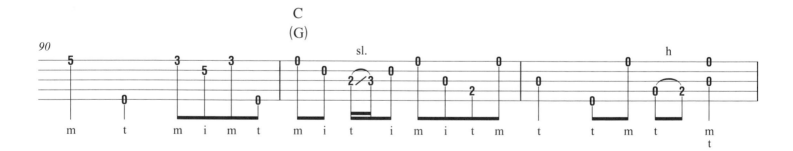

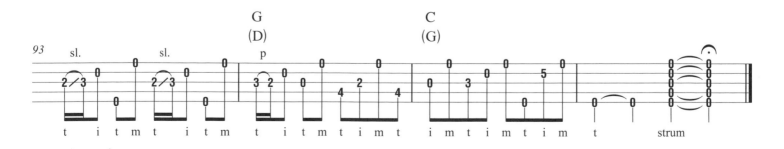

BANJO NOTATION LEGEND

TABLATURE graphically represents the banjo fingerboard. Each horizontal line represents a string, and each number represents a fret.

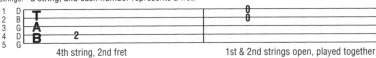

4th string, 2nd fret

1st & 2nd strings open, played together

TIME SIGNATURE:
The upper number indicates the number of beats per measure, the lower number indicates that a quarter note gets one beat.

CUT TIME:
Each note's time value should be cut in half. As a result, the music will be played twice as fast as it is written.

QUARTER NOTE:
time value = 1 beat

EIGHTH NOTES:
time value = 1/2 beat each

single   in series

SIXTEENTH NOTES:
time value = 1/4 beat each

single   in series

DOTTED QUARTER NOTE:
time value = 1 1/2 beat

TIE: Pick the 1st note only, then let it sustain for the combined time value.

TRIPLET: Three notes played in the same time normally occupied by two notes of the same time value.

GRACE NOTE: A quickly played note with no time value of its own. The grace note and the note following it only occupy the time value of the second note.

RITARD: A gradual slowing of the tempo or speed of the song.

QUARTER REST:
time value = 1 beat of silence

EIGHTH REST:
time value = 1/2 beat of silence

HALF REST:
time value = 2 beats of silence

WHOLE REST:
time value = 4 beats of silence

ENDINGS: When a repeated section has a first and second ending, play the first ending only the first time and play the second ending only the second time.

REPEAT SIGNS: Play the music between the repeat signs two times.

D.S. AL CODA:
Play through the music until you complete the measure labeled *"D.S. al Coda,"* then go back to the sign (%).
Then play until you complete the measure labeled *"To Coda ⊕,"* then skip to the section labeled " ⊕ Coda."

To Coda ⊕   *D.S. al Coda*   *⊕ Coda*

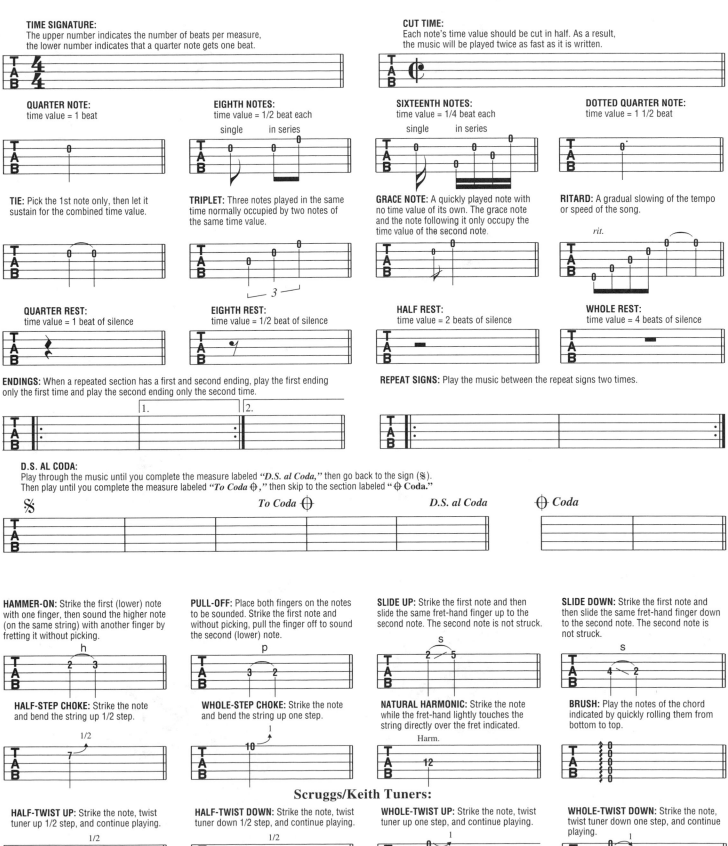

HAMMER-ON: Strike the first (lower) note with one finger, then sound the higher note (on the same string) with another finger by fretting it without picking.

PULL-OFF: Place both fingers on the notes to be sounded. Strike the first note and without picking, pull the finger off to sound the second (lower) note.

SLIDE UP: Strike the first note and then slide the same fret-hand finger up to the second note. The second note is not struck.

SLIDE DOWN: Strike the first note and then slide the same fret-hand finger down to the second note. The second note is not struck.

HALF-STEP CHOKE: Strike the note and bend the string up 1/2 step.

WHOLE-STEP CHOKE: Strike the note and bend the string up one step.

NATURAL HARMONIC: Strike the note while the fret-hand lightly touches the string directly over the fret indicated.

BRUSH: Play the notes of the chord indicated by quickly rolling them from bottom to top.

Scruggs/Keith Tuners:

HALF-TWIST UP: Strike the note, twist tuner up 1/2 step, and continue playing.

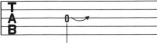

HALF-TWIST DOWN: Strike the note, twist tuner down 1/2 step, and continue playing.

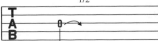

WHOLE-TWIST UP: Strike the note, twist tuner up one step, and continue playing.

WHOLE-TWIST DOWN: Strike the note, twist tuner down one step, and continue playing.

Right Hand Fingerings

t = thumb   i = index finger   m = middle finger

Hal Leonard Banjo Play-Along Series

1. BLUEGRASS
Ashland Breakdown • Deputy Dalton • Dixie Breakdown • Hickory Hollow • I Wish You Knew • I Wonder Where You Are Tonight • Love and Wealth • Salt Creek.

00102585 Book/CD Pack.........................$14.99

4. OLD-TIME CHRISTMAS
Away in a Manger • Hark! the Herald Angels Sing • Jingle Bells • Joy to the World • O Holy Night • O Little Town of Bethlehem • Silent Night • We Wish You a Merry Christmas.

00119889 Book/CD Pack.........................$14.99

The Banjo Play-Along Series will help you play your favorite songs quickly and easily with incredible backing tracks to help you sound like a bona fide pro! Just follow the banjo tab, listen to the demo track on the CD to hear how the banjo should sound, and then play along with the separate backing tracks. The CD is playable on any CD player and also is enhanced so Mac and PC users can adjust the recording to any tempo without changing the pitch! Each Banjo Play-Along pack features eight cream of the crop songs.

INCLUDES TAB

2. COUNTRY
East Bound and Down • Flowers on the Wall • Gentle on My Mind • Highway 40 Blues • If You've Got the Money (I've Got the Time) • Just Because • Take It Easy • You Are My Sunshine.

00105278 Book/CD Pack.........................$14.99

5. PETE SEEGER
Blue Skies • Get up and Go • If I Had a Hammer (The Hammer Song) • Kisses Sweeter Than Wine • Mbube (Wimoweh) • Sailing Down My Golden River • Turn! Turn! Turn! (To Everything There Is a Season) • We Shall Overcome.

00129699 Book/CD Pack.........................$17.99

3. FOLK/ROCK HITS
Ain't It Enough • The Cave • Forget the Flowers • Ho Hey • Little Lion Man • Live and Die • Switzerland • Wagon Wheel.

00119867 Book/CD Pack.........................$14.99

6. SONGS FOR BEGINNERS
Bill Cheatham • Black Mountain Rag • Cripple Creek • Grandfather's Clock • John Hardy • Nine Pound Hammer • Old Joe Clark • Will the Circle Be Unbroken.

00139751 Book/CD Pack.........................$14.99

HAL•LEONARD® CORPORATION
7777 W. BLUEMOUND RD. P.O. BOX 13819 MILWAUKEE, WI 53213

Prices, contents, and availability subject to change without notice.

www.halleonard.com

0915